"now you know me think more"

"now you know me think more"
A Journey with Autism using Facilitated Communication Techniques

Ppinder Hundal and Pauline Lukey

Jessica Kingsley Publishers
London and New York

BS

First published in the United Kingdom in 2003
by Jessica Kingsley Publishers Ltd
116 Pentonville Road
London N1 9JB, England
and
29 West 35th Street, 10th fl.
New York, NY 10001–2299, USA

www.jkp.com

Copyright ©2003 Ppinder Hundal and Pauline Lukey

Library of Congress Cataloging in Publication Data
A CIP catalog record for this book is available from the Library of Congress

British Library Cataloguing in Publication Data
A CIP catalogue record for this book is available from the British Library

ISBN 1 84310 144 0

Printed and Bound in Great Britain by
Athenaeum Press, Gateshead, Tyne and Wear

10/29/03

Dedicated to all people, struggling with the effects of autism, who are trying to make themselves understood.
In appreciation of the many people who have made this story possible and with special thanks to Sachi and Dorothy.

Contents

Pauline and Ppinder

Preface

This is the tale of an exciting journey that Ppinder and I have traveled together. Ppinder is handicapped by autism; she is non-verbal but is an eager communicator.

As a small girl she spoke a few baby words then, as happens so often with autism, she stopped talking. Life was very frustrating for her but now that she is able to communicate life is much easier and more rewarding.

This is the story of our communication journey and how our ability to communicate developed along the way.

For ease of understanding each of us has used a different type so that it is clear which of us is typing. Ppinder's typing is all in lower case letters and without punctuation because that is how she types.

The title of this book comes from one of the first statements Ppinder made. We hope that you will find our story interesting and that it may help others to try a similar journey.

Pauline and Ppinder

Our Journey

Ppinder

my name is ppinder

i don't talk so i have to use special
communication

how i communicate is with signs and
with facilitated communication

i have autism and that makes things
hard for me

to have autism is hard it makes the
words sound mixed

head is like i cant make me do what i
want

inside my head feels like there is a big
   hurt
sometimes i feel sad
about sad is i must be good
sometimes it is hard to be good then i
   feel sad
to be good means behave properly

Pauline

My name is Pauline. Ppinder and I met when
Ppinder was eight years old. Two years later,
when she was ten, she came to live with me
and we have learned together for many years.
These have been years of a great deal of
growth for both of us.

Ppinder is non-verbal and had no formal
way of communicating until some months
before she came to live with me.

When she was small she was fortunate to be
able to attend a day programme where chil-

dren with a variety of handicaps received preschool education; she then moved to a class for children with autistic behaviours. A group of parents of children with autism had formed one of the early societies, then known as the Victoria Society for Autistic Children. There was no special education in the school system for their children so they hired a teacher and began a class for the children in one of their homes. Once that was established they approached the local school board for help. The provincial social services ministry became involved and the class was incorporated into the school system in one of the elementary schools as a special needs class for children with autistic-like behaviours.

The school board provided the classroom, the teacher and two support workers and the Ministry of Social Services provided funding through a contract with the Society for additional support workers so that one-to-one support was available for the children. A management team was developed with a representative from the school district (the school psychologist), a social worker from the Ministry of Social Services and the President of the Victoria Society for Autistic Children.

The children travelled between their homes and school by a special bus service available to handicapped children. So began a very valuable collaboration that provided a Monday-to-Friday day programme for the education of the children and included support to help the parents develop the skills they needed. Saturday outings into the community expanded the children's experience with half of the children attending each week. Occasional overnight outings, including camping and a two-day visit to a farm, were enjoyable and valuable experiences. Regular staff meetings helped the staff refine individual children's programmes and weekly staff meetings with the psychologist helped the staff increase their skills.

Ppinder was very fortunate to be included in this innovative programme. Individual programmes were developed for each child including basic living skills, appropriate behaviour and concept development. Each child received individual instruction and was involved in small group participation every day. Ppinder was very timid and needed a great deal of encouragement to try a new task.

Like most of the children in the class Ppinder was non-verbal and had no formal way of communicating. When Ppinder was nine and a half years old sign language was introduced to the class. The sign language used is known as Signed English here in Canada and involves individual signs for words without spelling the word. In its complete form every word in a sentence is signed; however, for simplification just one word would be spoken and signed, and as the child progressed two signs might be put together. Some signs were modified so that all signs taught in those early days could be signed in such a way that the hand made contact with the body. This was done to help overcome the spatial difficulties which children with autism so often have.

A sign language instructor gave a one-hour class for the staff each week. Staff learned a few signs and learned how to gently shape the child's hand to make the sign while saying the word; also an object might be shown to the child to help clarify the sign's meaning. Individual strategies were developed to encourage each child.

For many of the children the first sign taught was "cookie". The staff worked individually with each child, first showing the cookie, then making the sign while saying the word and shaping the child's hand into the sign, then giving the child a small piece of cookie. This was repeated several times and the process repeated several times a day.

The children learned at very different rates so progress was individual. Each child first had to learn that this strange procedure meant something and to connect the position of the hand with the cookie. The staff watched for indications that the child was beginning to make an attempt to sign then praise was lavish and they quickly gave the piece of cookie while correcting the sign if this were needed.

Gradually new signs were introduced. The signs chosen were those which would be most useful and rewarding to the child as a way of getting something they wanted or accomplishing some daily task. The sign for "coat" was one of the early signs that provided opportunities for use as part of a routine daily activity –

the sign could be used when putting on or taking off the coat when going out of the classroom for outdoor activities and again when preparing to go home. At first the same staff member would work with the same child, then as the child became confident in using the signs, other staff members would begin to sign with the child.

Although Ppinder can hear, she has some hearing difficulties and can lip-read, but sometimes she mishears the first letter of a word. Sign language helps to clarify what she hears. It was anticipated that these children would be unlikely to live independent lives and long-term goals were developed with the parents. As those of you who have experience with autism know, caring for these children is very demanding.

It was decided that Ppinder needed intense ongoing support to develop to the best of her ability and that this could probably be best found in a special needs foster home. That was where Ppinder and I came into each other's lives. I had grown up in England where I had trained as a nurse and I had continued nursing after I emmigrated to Canada. I decided that I would like to change my direction and began university education with an interest in counselling and included several special needs education courses in my programme. Taking a break from studying, I worked in the class for autistic children and became fascinated with this interesting condition.

It was then that Ppinder and I first met and while I did not work with her individually I came to know her as a timid, winsome and frustrated little girl who was able to interact with staff and make some contact with a few of the other children. She was reluctant to try an activity independently and was reassured when she was involved in a familiar activity.

After further study I was looking for work and heard that a home was being sought for Ppinder where she could receive intensive instruction with a view to her eventually living in a group home.

Ppinder was ten years old when she came to live with me and so began a great change in both our lives. We lived in a small house with a garden where Ppinder enjoyed playing in water on the lawn in the summer; there was an apple tree with a swing which she also very much enjoyed. The house was only ten minutes' drive from Ppinder's school so was very convenient. As there were just the two of us I was able to centre our lives around Ppinder's needs and in this situation she flourished.

It was a big change for me. As a student I had been living alone in a bed-sitter; now I had a house and garden and a foster daughter and with this the great responsibility of finding how I could most easily help her.

For Ppinder there was even greater change and confusion as she came to me from her family home where she had lived with her parents and sister and brothers. She had many adjustments to make, not least the adjustment of living in a different culture. Ppinder's family had come to Canada from India before she was born, so she was used to living in a home where Punjabi was spoken, although she had of course become used to hearing English spoken at school. Another change for her was becoming used to a different diet.

By the time Ppinder came to live with me she knew four signs: "coat", "more", "cookie", "finish", and was able to make use of this small vocabulary to try to make herself understood.

After dinner on the second day she signed "coat", then "finish" to let me know that she wanted to go home. She was already beginning to use signs to make her wants known and to try to gain some control over her life.

As her ability to sign was limited she used other ways to try to communicate. If she wanted something to eat or drink she would lead me to the fridge and wait for me to take various items out to discover what she wanted. When I had chosen the correct item she would reach for it or lead me to the table. Other times she would get a utensil out of the cupboard before leading me to the fridge; I soon learned that she would always get an appropriate utensil and that gave me a guide to the kind of food she wanted. She was interested in watching me at work in the kitchen and her compulsion with order soon became apparent as she sorted the used cutlery and dishes and put them neatly along the back of the cabinet counter.

Like so many children with autism Ppinder had difficulty settling to sleep at night; this was difficult for me at first but I soon adjusted. She soon settled into our new routine as I tried to keep our days as predictable as possible. She enjoyed splashing the water while playing in the bath and when she had a bubble bath she liked to scoop the bubbles on the back of her hand and listen to the sound of the bubbles. Some years later when she was communicating clearly she told me that she likes to listen to the bubble music.

Ppinder was eager to learn. By the end of the first month of us living together she had learned two new signs and by the end of the following month four more signs. Gradually more words were added to her vocabulary and by the third month she had begun to put two signs together, first when she spontaneously signed, "want eat" and, soon after, "want home." She soon began to learn more quickly, adding about ten signs each month.

I encouraged her to sign by signing with her frequently and responding to her requests. I talked and signed about what we were doing and tried to make use of all suitable situations; for example at a mealtime when I thought she wanted more of something, I would ask her "Do you want more?" speaking the phrase and signing the word "more". I helped her to make the sign then gave her more. Other signs such as signs for objects or activities were easier to teach since I could do this by just showing her the object as I spoke and signed the word, or by demonstrating the activity, for example walking or jumping. I tried to give her sufficient time to assimilate a new sign before introducing another, gradually adding the signs that would be most useful to her. All of this was co-ordinated with the classroom activities.

At first I continued to shape her hand into the sign but after a month or two she was able to mimic the shape of my hand fairly accurately with just a little modification by me. Now she can usually learn a new sign by copying the sign demonstrated to her. I found that I had to modify my signs depending on our position. If we were side by side, as in the car, I could sign normally, but if we were facing each other I had to make a mirror image of the sign for her to learn to sign it correctly.

About a year after the sign language classes were started at school, she was able to understand and use forty signs and was putting words together to create new phrases including, "want more eat bread" and "drink want help please water". The order of the words was not always correct English grammar but the meaning was clear.

Gradually, Ppinder became more creative with her use of signs as she tried to make her wishes clear, for example she would sign "I want Ppinder good talk" and this meant that she wanted to be praised for what she was doing.

She occasionally created signs for words she didn't know, such as a row of buttons for pyjamas, and put two signs together to create one meaning – "light on" and "light off" are examples.

This was exciting as it demonstrated that she clearly understood that a sign was a symbol for a word or action. It was, however, confusing, as other people would not understand her self-made signs. I didn't want to discourage her so I accepted a few of these signs but at other times I would demonstrate the correct sign for that word. Ppinder enjoyed my reading illustrated children's book to her and while looking at the pictures I signed about what we were seeing. She often liked to look at these books alone and would sometimes sign to herself while looking at the book.

About a year after coming to live with me her acquisition of new signs slowed but there was increased clarity and complexity in her phrasing, such as "am finish I Ppinder want wash want bed".

Our lives became easier and she was able to express herself more clearly. I could understand her better and life for her was less frustrating as her wishes could be met more easily. Ppinder now knows about five hundred signs and uses many of them regularly. Over the years her use of sign language has become clearer and phrasing continues to become more sophisticated.

When Ppinder was sixteen we decided that this was the time for her to move to a group home. The goal when she came to live with me was to prepare for this and I thought that it would be better for her to move while she was a teenager than to wait until she was an adult. More services are available for children than for those aged nineteen and over, which is when they are classified as adults, so she would be likely to receive better support at this time. She moved to a group home with four other developmentally-handicapped teenagers and very caring group home parents, so again she was fortunate.

I was employed for three months to support the transition and after that continued to visit her frequently. Sometimes I would phone her and talk to her and one of the parents would tell me what she was signing. When she was nineteen she moved to a group home for adults. I provided respite care for her regularly for some time so we were able to keep in touch.

When Ppinder was twenty-three I heard that her social worker was looking for a new home for Ppinder, as the group home where she was living was no longer suitable. I contacted the social worker and Ppinder came to live with me again and we renewed our close relationship.

Eighteen months later Ppinder's communi-cation consultant and I heard about a technique to assist people with a wide range of handicaps to do things, including typing, which, without this supportive technique, they were unable to do. This was called Facilitated Communication (FC).

Ppinder had been interested in words for many years and clearly knew what letters words began with. She had used a typewriter with hand-over-hand guidance and progressed to being able to type regularly, without physical guidance, but with me telling her what letters to use.

When we first heard of FC it seemed obvious that Ppinder should be given an opportunity to try it. Her communication consultant learned a little about it, which she shared with me. We were told that we should determine whether Ppinder was left or right handed and use that hand. As Ppinder had already been typing with her right hand that was an easy decision.

Ppinder's communication consultant and I learned how to support Ppinder's hand with our hand cupped under her hand or arm and with a steady backward pressure to allow her to move her hand forward to the typewriter keys, then we would bring it back to the original position. One important part of the technique is that we must never push Ppinder's hand forward but must always maintain a backward pressure so that the choice of letter is always her's. The placement and strength of the support is very individual and becomes clear with practice. The goal is to have a steady rhythm to the typing, which we achieved after a rather jerky beginning. Over time the placement of the facilitator's supporting hand may change with experience and confidence.

It is important to get the help of someone experienced with FC before starting. There is a lot to learn and each person is different. Specific techniques may need to be modified to best suit the individual.

After learning something about the techniques to use Ppinder and I began a new phase in our amazing journey. We used the typewriter with which Ppinder was familiar and sat as before with the typewriter directly in front of her while I sat beside her. I had already told her about FC so when we were ready to start I explained again. I showed her how I would hold her hand and told her that this was how I would support her to make it easier for her and she could always let me know if she wanted to be held in a different way. I explained that she could choose what she wanted to type and I would lift her hand back after each letter so that she would be ready to type the next letter. I asked her if she wanted to try and she quickly signed "yes". I supported her hand, helping to keep her finger pointing firmly, and lifted her hand after each letter, but I did not guide her and no longer signed or spoke the words to be typed.

I had prepared a paper with five short phrases with the last word missing in each phrase. I read the phrase and Ppinder signed the missing word. I asked her to type the word and supported her hand, bringing it back to the starting position after each letter, but gave no additional help. As she completed each phrase I read the word she had typed then read the complete phrase.

Ppinder is good **gul** (girl)

Ppinder and Pauline drink **cofe**

Ppinder wants purple **bag**

Ppinder good time **cre** (car)

Do you want to type more **yes**

I asked her what more she wanted to type about. She signed a phrase then, with my support and encouragement, she slowly typed the words. Between each phrase I asked "any more?"

> **put clots pur bag** (put clothes purple
>
> bag)
>
> **good time and i want andy** (good time
>
> Andy I want Andy)
>
> **cloths pur ba bag** (clothes purple bag)
>
> **butfl drdxx bag** (beautiful dress bag)
>
> **c cuo wwhit vcaw** (Cathy white car)

Since she signed as well as typed I could understand even when the typed words were not always clear. At first, and for some time, I spoke the words she had signed, stressing each syllable. (Now I just read what she has typed or paraphrase it.) She likes to have her typing read back to her and she recently typed:

> **read the words then i can know what**
>
> **i write**

Learning to use FC was tiring and, at times, stressful for both Ppinder and me. Ppinder is very strong physically and often puts a lot of energy into her activities; she typed with this same strong energy as she moved to select the letters and I had to use strong pressure to hold back her hand. As she became comfortable with this new method of communicating she gradually relaxed and her movements became softer and rhythmic.

When we started FC Ppinder needed me to place her hand on mine with her fingers folded into my palm and my index finger supporting her index finger to keep it firm. I have been able to change the support for Ppinder to her wrist then to her forearm or elbow. The amount of support needed depends upon how she is feeling and some days she can type successfully with the support at her elbow or occasionally at the shoulder (see photos of FC support).

We have found that if her facilitator is sitting close to her and they are in physical contact she can sometimes type with the facilitator just holding a fold of her sleeve.

Support to hand and pointing finger

Our hope is that Ppinder will eventually be able to type independently with the facilitator close to her but not touching her. When we first talked to her about typing independently she was not willing to try but now she says that maybe she will be able to type alone someday. She has, on a few occasions, initiated typing a message independently but she obviously appreciates the reassurance of a facilitator. She is however able to point to familiar words independently and to point independently to her choice between two or three written options offered her.

Support to hand

Support at wrist

Support holding sleeve

Independent

As well as using a typewriter Ppinder is quite comfortable using a computer and also a letter board, which is a replica of a keyboard with some useful words added. She has had no difficulty with transitions between the various pieces of equipment and uses them with equal ease, using whichever is most convenient at the time.

1	2	3	4	5	6	7	8	9	0
Q	W	E	R	T	Y	U	I	O	P
A	S	D	F	G	H	J	K	L	
Z	X	C	V	B	N	M	HEADACHE		
MORE		SPACE					STOP		
YES	NO	MAYBE		SOMETHING ELSE		FINISH			

Ppinder's letter board

When we began only Ppinder's communication consultant and I were her facilitators. Our goal is that all people in regular contact with Ppinder will be able to facilitate her and now her caregiver and the staff at her day programme also facilitate her successfully. Ppinder has initiated helping new facilitators learn how to give her the support she needs. Sometimes she is particularly sensitive to touch and we have to be sure that her arm is covered by her sleeve.

We continued daily, typing short phrases of Ppinder's choice, or in response to my suggestions of a topic. From the beginning she used the space bar correctly. Sometimes she typed without looking at the keyboard and at times seemed to be deliberately letting me know that she didn't need to look, although occasionally she hit the key next to the one needed.

She would frequently type one phrase while signing another and sometimes she would start with groups of letters which were not recognizable words, then words would appear after these.

Later she began with a familiar phrase or a phrase which I had suggested. I still sometimes suggest a phrase that will give her a starting point. For example, I may say, "can you tell me about…" and she will reply "**about…**" However, now she usually begins with what she wants to say.

She has always liked to type the first letter of a word and expect us to know what she means. This still happens occasionally, and then we remind her to type the whole word.

At first the spelling was phonetic but then both spelling and phrasing spontaneously improved.

Two days after beginning she typed:

lois wrt car (Lois white car)

do gren bath (Dorothy green bath)

gud tn tiping (good time typing)

Four months later:

to mum mum cook diner eat diner

butiful dinner cofe

Three-and-a-half months after this:

we go swim I had good time in hot

pool

Days when Ppinder was calm were more successful. Now she can be successful even when she is tense, but it is obviously more difficult for her then.

Six months after we started we watched a video of people using FC – this was a red-letter day. Ppinder had a great deal of difficulty getting started, then typed

think now you no me think more

ggggive me time to have how i can

get ther how i must be good girl

This was an emotional day for both of us.

I tried and continue to try to let her go at her own pace, providing her with opportunities but not pushing her. I frequently encourage her to continue by asking "any more?" I don't ask her to use punctuation or capital letters, it seems more important to have her say what she wants without any pressure. After all it is communication that is important, not correct grammar.

A year after we stated using FC Ppinder got a Canon Communicator, she was delighted and took another step forward.

> pauline gave me little typewriter
>
> i like the new typewriter
>
> ppinder can type more on the
>
>   typewriter
>
> first i can have the words i want and
>
>   then i ttype
>
> the pink bag and get the bag

She began to make requests and comments more clearly.

> pauline put the tree in the room
>
>   tdhen it will be crismas
>
> then i can have bubbles under the
>
>   tree

She also began to tell me about events in her life, like the day she got stuck in the elevator alone, and to clarify when I didn't understand.

> we go to the werkshop and i go for
>
>   coffee

elevator treat hard then man open

door properlilly

can i have coffee tomoro

I asked her if she could explain "treat hard."

elefater tret hard is elevator wont do

what i want

In 1994 Ppinder and I went to an International Conference on Autism in Toronto. It was very exciting and we both had a very good time.

we went to td Toronto and we

stayed at a hotel

i go to the pool and i swim better

pool

other i did was have hot choklet in

hotel room and toast and man

come get dishes

more is we go in plane and i see snow

pauline says it was clowds

After we returned home we listened to some of the tapes we got at the conference. Ppinder was particularly interested when we listened to Jim Sinclair's presentation and I told her he is autistic. I told her how he wishes to be accepted as who he is and calls himself autistic rather than saying he has an autism spectrum disorder. He is a wonderful advocate. His presentation was titled "Don't mourn for us". It was a plea to parents to accept their children as they are. He believes that their mourning is for the child they expected but did not get rather than for the child they do have. He spoke about his philosophy and what autism is like for him. He spoke of the many sensory distortions which effect him, the discomfort of his body and the pain often associated with eating. In response to one mother's question about her four-year-old son screaming when his hair was cut he said it was painful to have his hair cut and now he usually cuts his own hair. Ppinder listened intently then typed:

the man is autistic like me i can try

get put like the man then i could

talk

As well as longing to talk Ppinder would like to read and write. Although she sometimes writes using FC techniques, it is not easy for her and the legibility varies.

As time went on Ppinder showed more sophistication in her typing and her ability to maintain sequential thought also became apparent.

first i want to read the writing then

we can get the bag ready

how can i get the purple bag ready

maybe i can wait until pauline has

done the laundry

With facilitation Ppinder has been able to tell us so much about her life – before, we had to guess what was going on for her. Conversations have become easier and helpful, as shown in this conversation with Dorothy, Ppinder's communication consultant.

Dorothy: Can you tell me why you don't want to take your medicine?

Ppinder: i don't want the pills because they make me feel tired and sick

Dorothy: Where do you feel the sickness?

Ppinder: i feel sick in my stomake

Dorothy: Would it be better after dinner?

Ppinder: after dinner may be better

Dorothy: Anything special at work today?

Ppinder: i did have a treet at workshop today for valentines day

Dorothy: Do you think that facilitation helps you?

Ppinder: i think that facilitation helps me think what i need to say

Unconnected strings of letters are sometimes a feature of Ppinder's typing. These letters are usually associated with the topics on which she perseverates. One day I asked her about this and she confirmed my suspicions that sometimes two conversations are going on at the same time – one about a chosen topic and the other from her automatic perseverative repertoire.

With increased confidence has come increased competence and an ability to participate more fully in life. For the first time Ppinder has participated actively in her personal service plan meeting. Before the meeting Ppinder and her communication consultant met to discuss the topics that would be reviewed and Ppinder prepared her ideas. Ppinder still had opportunities to provide input during the meeting. At recent medication review meetings Ppinder answered the psychiatrist's questions herself – a big step from someone else answering with what they hoped were the correct answers.

All of these changes have been incredibly exciting – at times almost impossible for me to believe.

One particularly exciting time was when Ppinder and another autistic woman met to converse using their laptops. They had known each other for at least twenty-five years and were finally able to sit down together and have a conversation, providing each other with support for their difficulties. A very moving experience for this writer.

Some time ago I decided that it was time for me to begin to retire and Ppinder moved to a new home, she now comes to me for two weekends a month.

Ppinder has many of the usual autistic characteristics and change, unexpected events, loud noise and empty time when she doesn't know what to do cause her a great deal of stress. To make life easier for her there is a routine pattern for most of her days. She lives at home Monday to Friday and at weekends goes to respite care to provide a break for her caregiver. This also gives Ppinder a more varied life. She spends every other weekend with me and the alternate weekends goes to another home.

We try to keep the daily care routines in her life the same in the three homes but there are other activities which are unique to each. One major difference is that Monday to Friday she goes to a day programme at the Garth Homer Centre while at weekends she is at home all day except for any outings we may plan. Ppinder needs periods of quiet time to prevent the build up of too much stress. She likes to take many rests. After she has started her day with breakfast and washed and dressed, she lies on her bed for a while.

Ppinder travels to the day programme by the Handy Dart bus service, which is a local bus service for people who are unable to travel by the regular bus. Direct transportation between her home and day programme is provided.

The Garth Homer Centre provides a wide range of services for people with a wide range of disabilities. Ppinder is enrolled in the STARR programme where the emphasis is on Self-esteem Through Acceptance, Respect and Responsibility. When Ppinder arrives she hangs up her coat in the hallway, then goes into the activity room where she is greeted by her worker and usually enjoys a cup of tea or coffee.

Ppinder is able to tolerate only a limited amount of stimulation without becoming stressed, so throughout the day she has regular rest periods alone in a quiet room. After her first rest she joins her worker and they plan Ppinder's schedule of activities so that Ppinder knows what to expect. This schedule changes from time to time and includes activities at Ppinder's workstation, which is by a window in a quiet corner of the room, and activities out of the centre. Sometimes she carries out office tasks such as shredding paper, stamping, folding and stuffing envelopes. She also participates in projects involving sewing, folding fabrics, sorting boxes and bags, painting, and sticking and gluing collages. Ppinder enjoys swimming once a week and other days she and her worker may go for a drive to a pleasant green space for a refreshing, calming walk. Helping at a petting zoo in the summer, where she has been involved in various activities including cleaning the goat shed and brushing the goats, has been a pleasurable and useful experience for her.

Her programme sometimes includes making her lunch once a week and she and her worker will shop for the ingredients then prepare the meal. For this she needs varying amounts of help but she is very good at clearing up and putting the used items away. Other days she takes her lunch from home.

Each member of the staff that works with Ppinder is able to use sign language and to facilitate her communication using FC. One very exciting day a few years ago was awards day when Ppinder received the award for most improvement that year.

Ppinder receiving prize

zainum talked then gave me the

award

the award was a fish and i got a pink

bag and i got a certificat

the award was for good work

i felt very proud to get the award

At weekends Ppinder's activities vary. At one of the respite homes she often goes for outings with her respite caregiver and they may go for a walk at one of the many parks or beaches in the area. The weekends that Ppinder spends with me provide opportunities for her to unwind and she often spends many hours in bed. She is refreshed after this quiet time and ready to get back to her other regular activities.

Ppinder's favourite hobby is collecting bags. She likes any type of bag and has many in sizes ranging from small change purses to large duffel bags. Some she uses in daily life while others are displayed in her bedroom much to her delight. Ppinder also likes to look at books, catalogues and magazines and has told us, by using FC, that *The Reader's Digest* is her favourite. While she sometimes likes to listen to music, her over-sensitivity to sound means that it must be very quiet so that it is not stressful. Occasionally a former staff member at the Garth Homer Centre goes in to play his guitar and Ppinder enjoys this a great deal. She also likes to sit quietly and watch what is going on around her and while she may not want to participate actively I believe that she is very involved in what is going on in her world.

She is interested in words and often asks me to write and then read what I have written. I write about what we have been doing, or about events that have happened in Ppinder's life and always include some words that she can recognize. She often likes to sign the words she recognizes.

Ppinder has a very good dress sense. When she lived with me she liked to suggest what I should wear and her choices were always very harmonious. Her favourite colours are pink and shades of mauve and purple.

Her favourite foods include cheese and cheese dishes, as well as eggs and curried dishes. She especially likes chocolate and coffee and usually likes juices which are red, pink or purple.

Ppinder is interested in hearing about other autistic people. When she saw a picture of the author Donna Williams and I told her that Donna is autistic her face lit up and she was eager for me to read some of Donna's writings to her.

At the beginning we didn't know anyone using the Facilitated Communication technique so we were in unknown territory. There was a lot of uncertainty – uncertainty about what was happening, uncertainty about whether Ppinder was choosing the words or whether I was unconsciously guiding her. Sometimes she seemed to be typing my thoughts – as I know her so well it was difficult not to anticipate what she was going to say. Although some typing indicated that I was not guiding her I was not at first convinced that they really were her words.

When public disbelief became an issue I had to look at what shaped my belief in the validity of Facilitated Communication. I believe that I do sometimes influence what Ppinder types, but this is not surprising – we all influence others in our conversations. I don't know how much influence there is nor do I understand how that influence happens. I also know that I am not deliberately guiding her and am sure that she is selecting the letters.

What convinces me that Ppinder is choosing the words?

- She types independently or almost independently.

- I can feel the strength of Ppinder's hand moving to the letters as she types.

- Sometimes, particularly on sensitive issues, she chooses to use my finger to type, so I can easily feel that she is in control.

- She reacts emotionally when typing about sensitive topics.

- Using facilitation she has given many of her facilitators information which they had not previously known.

Ppinder is able to express herself much more fully than before FC and while communication is still somewhat limited it is much more complete and meaningful. Since the advent of FC and greater insight into Ppinder's abilities there has been a remarkable change in her life. Before FC I was sure that Ppinder understood much more than she could demonstrate. Now she has proved her understanding and other people see her with new eyes.

We hope that our experiences will help others to understand a little more about autism and about FC, that it will assist facilitators, and that it will provide encouragement to those who are trying to communicate.

Here are some thoughts about FC and how to get started.

- Get the help and support of those who have experience with FC.

- Remember that FC is not just about typing. It is a technique used to assist a person to make a choice which, without that assistance, they would not be able to make.

- While it is natural to have some doubts, as facilitators we must approach FC with open minds. The person learning to use FC must have our respect and support and the decision to try should be theirs.

- Be genuine in any requests or questions you ask. Never ask trick questions or try to prove whether the response is genuine.

- Have an open mind and be prepared to be pleasantly surprised from time to time.

  - help type first give the typewriter then help

  - the people should know that it is good to be typing

  - then people can get what they want

  - tell people with autism that they can learn to type i can type because i

know the words in my head then
my head have how i type

• i can say what i want and then other
people understand

• we can read the words then i know
what i write when the words are on
the paper then we can read

• i want you to know that i am smart

Resources

United Kingdom and Europe

L'Arche UK
10 Briggate
Silsden
Keighley
W. Yorkshire BD20 9JT
UK
Phone: ++44 (0) 1535 656186
Fax: ++44 (0) 1535 656426
Email: info@larche.org.uk
Web: www.larche.org.uk

Autism Europe
Avenue E. Van Becelaere 26b, bte 21
B-1170 Brussels
Belgium
Phone: ++32 (0) 2 675 75 05
Email: president@autismeurope.org
Web: www.autismeurope.org

Autism Research Unit
School of Sciences
University of Sunderland
Sunderland SR2 7EE
UK
Phone: ++44 (0) 191 510 8922
Web: http://osiris.sunderland.ac.uk/autism/

European Disability Forum
Rue du Commerce 39–41
B-1000 Brussels
Belgium
Phone: ++32 (0) 2 282 46 09
Email: info@edf-feph.org
Web: www.edf-feph.org/en/welcome.htm

Andy Grayson
(Researcher in field of Facilitated Communication)
Centre for Childhood, Development and Learning
Faculty of Education and Language Studies
The Open University
Walton Hall, Milton Keynes MK7 6AA
UK
Phone: ++44 (0) 1908 653295
Fax: ++44 (0) 1908 654111
Email: a.grayson@open.ac.uk

The Irish Society for Autism
Unity Building
16/17 Lower O'Connell Street
Dublin
Ireland
Phone: ++353 (0) 1 874 4684
Fax: ++353 (0) 1 874 4224
Email: autism@isa.iol.ie
Web: www.iol.ie/~dary/isa

The National Autistic Society
393 City Road
London EC1V 1NG
UK
Phone: ++44 (0) 207 833 2299
Fax: ++44 (0) 207 833 9666
Email: nas@nas.org.uk
Web: www.nas.org.uk

Parents and Professionals and Autism (PAPA) Resource Centre
Donard House
Knockbracken Healthcare Park
Saintfield Road
Belfast BT8 8BH
Northern Ireland
UK
Phone: ++44 (0) 289 040 1729
Fax: ++44 (0) 289 040 3467
Email: info@autismni.org
Web: www.autismni.org

The Scottish Society for Autism
Hilton House
Alloa Business Park
Whins Road
Alloa FK10 3SA
UK
Phone: ++44 (0) 1259 720044
Fax: ++44 (0) 1259 720051
Web: www.autism-in-scotland.org.uk

Ta Main Pour Parler (TMPP)
(The Association for the Enhancement of Facilitated
Communication)
2 rue de Saint Cloud
92150 Suresnes
France
Phone: ++33 (0) 1 45 06 79 36
Fax: ++33 (0) 1 45 06 79 36
Web: www.tmpp.net

USA

L'Arche USA
Phone: ++1 (1) 206 306 1330
Fax: ++1 (1) 206 306 1329
Email: chimos@aol.com
Website: www.larcheusa.org/index.htm

Asperger Syndrome Coalition of the US
PO Box 351268
Jacksonville, FL 32235-1268
Phone: ++1 (1) 866 4ASPRGR
Website: www.asperger.org

Autism Research Institute
4182 Adams Avenue
San Diego, CA 92116
Fax: ++1 (1) 619 563 6840
Web: www.autism.com/ari

Autism Society of America
7910 Woodmont Avenue, Suite 300
Bethesda, MD 20814-3067
Phone: ++1 (1) 301 657 0881
Email: info@autism-society.org
Web: www.autism-society.org

Center for the Study of Autism
PO Box 4538
Salem, OR 97302
www.autism.org

The Doug Flutie Jr. Foundation for Autism
(Doug Flutie is an American football star who has an
Autistic son)
233 Cochituate Road 2nd Floor
PO Box 767
Framingham, MA 01701
Phone: ++1 (1) 508 270 8855
Fax: ++1 (1) 508 270 6868
Email: info@dougflutiejrfoundation.org
Web: www.dougflutiejrfoundation.org

Facilitated Communication Coalition of Indiana
Indiana Institute on Disability and Community
2853 East 10th Street
Bloomington, IN 47408-2601
Web: www.bloomington.in.us/~fcindy/

Facilitated Communication Institute
Syracuse University
370 Huntington Hall
Syracuse NY 13244-2340
Phone: ++1 (1) 315 443 9657
Email: fcstaff@sued.syr.edu
Web: http://soeweb.syr.edu/thefci

Facilitated Communication Project Phoenix Arizona
Web: http://aztec.asu.edu/fcproj/

Vermont Facilitated Communication Network
Facilitated Communication
Division of Developmental Services
103 South Main Street
Waterbury, VT 05617-1601
Phone: ++1 (1) 802 241 2644
Fax: ++1 (1) 802 241 4224
Web: www.uvm.edu/~uapvt/faccom.html

Canada

L'Arche Canada
381, Rachel Est
Montreal, QC H2W 1E8
Phone: ++1 (1) 514 844 1661
Fax: ++1 (1) 514 844 1960
Email: office@larchecanada.org
Web: www.larchecanada.org

Autism Society of Canada
PO Box 65
Orangeville, Ontario L9W 2Z5
Phone: ++1 (1) 519 942 8720
Fax: ++1 (1) 519 942 3566
Email: info@autismsocietycanada.ca
Web: www.autismsocietycanada.ca

Autism Society of British Columbia
301–3701 East Hastings Street
Burnaby, BC V5C 2H6
Phone: ++1 (1) 604 434 0880
Fax: ++1 (1) 604 434 0801
Email: info@autismbc.ca
Web: www.autismbc.ca

Autism Treatment Services of Canada
404–94th Avenue SE
Calgary, Alberta T2J 0E8
Phone: ++1 (1) 403 253 6961
Email: atsc@autism.ca
Web: www.autism.ca

Garth Homer Society
(Ppinder's day programme)
813 Darwin Avenue
Victoria, BC V8X 2X7
Phone: ++1 (1) 250 475 2270
Email: ghomer@garthhomersociety.org
Web: www.garthhomersociety.org

Geneva Centre for Autism
250 Davisville Avenue Suite 200
Toronto, Ontario M4S H2L
Phone: ++1 (1) 416 322 7877
Email: info@autism.net
Web: www.autism.net

International Society for Augmentative
and Alternative Communication – ISAAC
49 The Donway West, Suite 308
Toronto, Ontario M3C 3M9
Phone: ++1 (1) 416 385 0351
Fax: ++1 (1) 416 385 0351
Email: secretatiat@isaac-online.org
Web: www.isaac-online.org

Kerry's Place Autism Services
34 Berczy Street
Aurora, Ontario L4G 1W9
Phone: ++1 (1) 905 841 6611
Fax: ++1 (1) 905 841 1461
Web: www.kerrysplace.com

Parent Books
(Internet bookstore recommended by the Geneva Centre)
201 Harbord Street
Toronto, Ontario M5S 1H6
Phone: ++1 (1) 416 537 8334
Fax: ++1 (1) 416 537 9499
Email: Inquiry: info@parentbooks.ca
Sales: orders@parentbooks.ca
Web: www.parentbookstore.com

Australia and New Zealand

L'Arche Australia
31 Girrabong Road
Lenah Valley
TAS 7008
Australia
Phone: ++61 (0) 362 781 883
Fax: ++61 (0) 362 783 983

Autism Victoria
PO Box 235
Ashburton
Victoria 3147
Australia
Phone: ++61 (0) 398 850 533
Email: admin@autismvictoria.org.au
Web: www.autismvictoria.org.au

Book in Hand Bookshop
(Book in Hand Bookshop specialises in books on autism,
including books on Facilitated Communication.)
Web: www.bookinhand.com.au

Cloud 9 Children's Foundation
PO Box 30979
Lower Hutt
Wellington
New Zealand
Phone: ++64 (0) 492 09473
Email: foundation@entercloud9.com
Web: www.withyoueverystepoftheway.com

DEAL Communications Centre Inc.
538 Dandenong Road
Caulfield
Victoria 3162
Australia
Contact: Rosemary Crossley
Phone: ++61 (0) 395 096 324
Email: dealcc@vicnet.net.au
Web: http://home.vicnet.net.au/~dealcc/welcome.htm